ISBN 978-1-331-32677-9
PIBN 10174739

1 MONTH OF
FREE
READING

at
www.ForgottenBooks.com

By purchasing this book you are eligible for one month membership to ForgottenBooks.com, giving you unlimited access to our entire collection of over 700,000 titles via our web site and mobile apps.

To claim your free month visit:

www.forgottenbooks.com/free174739

English
Français
Deutsche
Italiano
Español
Português

www.forgottenbooks.com

Mythology Photography **Fiction**
Fishing Christianity **Art** Cooking
Essays Buddhism Freemasonry
Medicine **Biology** Music **Ancient
Egypt** Evolution Carpentry Physics
Dance Geology **Mathematics** Fitness
Shakespeare **Folklore** Yoga Marketing
Confidence Immortality Biographies
Poetry **Psychology** Witchcraft
Electronics Chemistry History **Law**
Accounting **Philosophy** Anthropology
Alchemy Drama Quantum Mechanics
Atheism Sexual Health **Ancient History**
Entrepreneurship Languages Sport
Paleontology Needlework Islam
Metaphysics Investment Archaeology
Parenting Statistics Criminology
Motivational

Memories O' Hame

and

Other Poems

BY

William McCormack

With Biographical Sketches by

JOHN McNEIL, M. E.

and

ALEXANDER LAIRD, LITT. D.

Errata

Page 34 line 13 read "Wave beat shore."
  "   60 "   3 " "I pu'd the brambles, etc."
  "   73 "   6 " "border for bordee."
  "   73 "   7 " "see for ser."
  "   76 " 10 " "lilt for lit."
  "   76 " 14 " "Greenock for Ceenock."
  "   77 " last word read "diel" for kiel.
  "   96 "   2 read "Lawhull" for Lawhaull.
  "   97 top line read "whit" for white.
  "   97 line 10 read "wondrous" for wrondous.

Foreword

IN response to the request of Mrs. McCormack and her family it has given me great pleasure indeed, to carefully read over and select from the poetical productions f her late gifted and honoured husband the contents of this ttle volume.

In making the selections, I have endeavored to give the ream of Mr. McCormack's musings, and have only made 1ch changes, as I am sure he would have approved, could e have been consulted in the matter. If those who read "Memries O' Hame" and other poems, derive as much pleasure nd profit by doing so, as I have in preparing them for the ress, they will indeed be happy.

ALEXANDER LAIRD.

ʃildwood, New Jersey,
March 1st, 1915.

Memoir of

MR. WILLIAM McCORMACK

BY

JOHN McNEIL, M. E., Denver, Colorado.

TO WRITE or speak of the reverance—the respect and the tender affection I possess for the late Mr. William McCormack is a difficult task indeed; of his accomplishments, or the unbounded pleasure that was mine, as in deep, sweet converse I walked arm in arm with him, my gifted companion of thirty years, my pen—my lips, fail in their eloquence to adequately portray. But, unworthy as I may be to perform the task—by special request—assigned me, yet mine be the sacred duty and sweet pleasure of recalling, at least some of the sterling virtues, estimable qualities and personal charms of my beloved, lifelong friend and fellow countryman; and, if I cannot crown his genius with a wreath of justice, I shall at least offer from my heart a garland of love in this brief memoir, made up from reminiscenses of his own lofty feelings and sublime inspirations, which so often touched tender chords within my heart.

I shall speak of Mr. McCormack in no cold, ordinary measured terms, believing with all my heart that he has "well earned a niche in the Temple of Fame," with modern Scottish Poets.

Like many men, who have made a name for themselves, William McCormack owed much to the early training and example of his "douce" God-fearing parents, hence the deep affection which he ever manifested towards them. Doubtless he had his faults, for, "the best of men are only the least sinful." But, as far as I knew him—and few knew him better—there were no serious blemishes to mar his manly character in its entirety. He had a warm, unselfish, loving heart, unseared by sordid thoughts, or soured by harking care, or, he never could have enjoyed the pleasure of such chaste fancy to sing so sweetly. Mr. McCormack was an ardent reader, and was gifted with a wonderful memory. His intellect was acute, rather than strong; brilliant, rather than profound. If his life had been prolonged it was his intention to have devoted much of his time to literature. But, that was not God's will. Beyond such schooling as he obtained prior to reaching the age of ten, and by an occasional attendance afterwards at a night school, he was self-taught. It was by sheer force of application, and in the face of many difficulties that he improved his mind, and developed his literary tastes, bringing himself out from the seclusion of obscurity into a position of at least, local influence and honour.

He was a close student of Scottish folk-lore and history, and as such was honoured by those who knew him. His ability to accurately recall historic events, give dates and narrate facts relating to the history of his native land, was truly marvelous. Few men, either at home or abroad, were more conversant with Scottish life and customs, past and present, than Mr. McCormack. He was wonderfully familiar with the green glades, the heather moors, the woody groves, the ferny glens and the rippling streams of his native Shire; deeming them charmingly picturesque and enchantingly lovely; thus we find him often singing of their peculiar charms, their rural beauty and sweet fragrance in such sweet poems as the following:

"Beside the Calder," "The Shotts" and "Bonkle,"
Where he Leeved as a Bairnie Langsyne."

"I hae leeved in this worl for full fifty years
'Midst its joys, its sorrows, its smiles and its tears,
And th'ae magic word ever sweet tae ma ears—
Is hame wi its mem'ries and thochts,
It tiches ma hert like some saft melodie'
That I've heard lang syne by a fond mother's knee,
And again I'm a bairn 'neth that humble rif-tree,
By the road-side no faur frae th' Shotts."

Like beautiful scenery, that we sometimes find in solitary cannons, hidden far from the beaten paths of men, so we often find the best and most lovable types of mankind in the humblest walks of life, far removed from the busy haunts of men. The life of my dear departed friend, William McCormack, was a striking example of this. He entered the coal mines at Newmains, Scotland, at the tender age of ten years, but, on reaching manhood, became a mechanical engineer, and for nearly forty years he worked at his trade, most of that time being in charge of machinery about coal and metalliferous mines. Being an excellent tradesman, as well as a noble and lovable man, he was highly respected by his employers and 'looked up to" by his fellow-workmen. He was in love with his calling, for while he had certainly talent to rise above it, he was always happy and contented in it.

In a cleanly swept engine room, surrounded with brightly, shining machinery, and wearing his newly washed overalls he was unfailingly happy; to me it was a source of great pleasure to meet him there: and there too were some of his best poems conceived and composed. He would hum the composition of his words over in his leisure moments to some "Auld Scotch Air," and when relieved from duty and seated by his 'ain cosy, clean fiesride," he would reduce them to writing. No man was ever fonder of home and family than William

McCormack. Of his tidy, thrifty Scotch wife, he would say to me: "Ma wee wife Teenie, cooks an' keeps a' things tidy, an' pleases me better than ony ither hoose-keeper I ken." His delicacy of thought, fertility of imagination, and felicity of expression, so clear, so simple and so fresh in utterance, were to me as refreshingly sweet as the fragrance of the flowery verdure of the hills and the valleys o'er which we roamed together; his pathos, tender and refined, went direct to the heart. The untiring grandeur and beauty of the all-enduring storied piles, and the illimitable sweep of Colorado's Rocky mountains, with their caps of perpetual snow, never ceased to have a strong facination for his impassioned heart. He exhibited a deep love for, and a high appreciation of the charms of natural scenery, and his descriptive, conversational powers in depicting the varied beauty of landscape, the grandeur of the hills, the rushing streams, the wild flowers and waving pines, were the breathings of a pure and exalted soul, which are now to his sacred memory, enshrined within my heart as never—fading immortelles.

When our hands clasped last, with hearty grasp,
We little dreamt, 'twould be the last
In life, between you and I, old friend,
    Between you and I.
But gazing now, through the mist of tears,
My boon companion of thiry years,
Lies cold and voiceless—dead, departed friend,
    Lies cold and voiceless—dead.
In the somber hush of the graveyard's gloom,
When I saw thy silent form laid in the tomb,
My heart ached to its inmost core, lost friend,
    My heart ached to its inmost core.
To realize that thou, and thy precious "flow of soul"
Were adown the "Deathless Valley," beyond this earthly
    goal.

Here, ever lost to me, my beloved friend,
     Here, ever lost to me.
Oh ! vanished joy, I sadly mourn
For thee, true comrade, beyond the bourne,
Thy passing I deplore, real friend,
     Thy passing I deplore.
But tho' pierced by grief's keenest dart,
God's precious promise soothes my heart,
To know we'll meet again--joyous friends,
     To know we'll meet again.

BIOGRAPHICAL SKETCH

BY

Rev. Alexander Laird, Ph. D., Litt. D.

To me, it has been an esteemed privilege, as well as a highly appreciated honour to respond to the request to furnish the readers of this little volume of poetical gems, with a brief sketch of their gifted author.

My recollections of the late William McCormack, run away back through four and a half decades—to the time when I was a lad, and he a young man.

Mr. McCormack was born at Gasswater, Ayrshire, Scotland, on the tenth day of May, 1851, and eleven months later was brought by his parents to Newmains, Lanarkshire, where the happy years of his childhood, boyhood and early manhood were spent. At the tender age of ten, he became a pit-laddie, toiling for over ten hours each day in the bowels of the earth, devoting most of his evenings by his mother's clean, warm fireside, or in the Newmains night-school, reading wholesome literature and studying subjects of a practical character. From an examination of the copy book which he used in the Newmains night-school in 1864, I find that as a mere lad he possessed marked literary taste and general ability away above the average. Ere he had reached his majority he had worked himself out of the mines, and was acting in the capacity of winding engineman at one of the mines in

Newmains. About the year 1876, he began contributing verse to the local newspapers, particularly the Hamilton Advertiser, and from that period up to the time of his death, wherever he was, he was sensitive to the touch of the muse, and the contents of this little volume tell how naturally and how sweetly he could sing.

In 1885 Mr. McCormack came to America, settling in the State of Colorado, where he spent twenty happy and useful years. Because, like Scotland's great singer, Robert Burns, he could not witness "man's inhumanity to man," without expressing his indignation in verse: he was forced to seek employment beyond the State of Colorado, which he loved so well. In 1904, he accepted of a position in Mexico, where he remained and prospered for over nine years, until forced by the Mexican War to get out of the danger zone. In July of last year, 1914, he returned to the suburbs of Denver, Colorado, where he proposed spending the evening of his li e, cultivating his gift of the muse, and following literary pursuits; but his twilight was short; he was only back in Colorado, two months, when after a few days suffering, God took him home, leaving in sorrow behind, his widow, two sons, one daughter, and a host of warm, loyal friends. William McCormack was in the fullest and truest sense of the word a typical Scot. In spite of his long residence in the United States and his unswerving loyalty to its institutions, he retained with a tenderness that was touching, his love for his native land, which can be traced like a golden thread, running through almost everything he wrote.

In a long letter which I received from him, less than a year ago, while he was still in Mexico, he said: "I have been home in Scotland twice, in 1891 and in 1912. If I thought I was going to die in a year, I would start for the old land again tomorrow." How unassuming he was in relation to his poetic genius and literary qualifications! To show this, I quote from another of his letters now open before me. "I am flattered", he writes, "that you should have noticed my verses in the Hamilton Advertiser. I am well aware that there is no great merit in them, but even the wild birds of the forest have not all the same gift of song. I do the best I can with the little gift I have, never forcing myself to write anything at any time, for the muse must be wooed gently—she will not be coerced. While a great deal is made of the influence of environment the true poet is found anywhere, he can soar above the most prosaic surroundings."

Had Mr. McCormack been spared for a few years longer he would undoubtedly have added to the laurels which were already his.

In deciding to publish her lamented and gifted husband's poems, Mrs. McCormack is not only perpetuating his memory, but is at the same time furnishing those who knew him in life and all others who may read his musings on "Hame" and other subjects with many a pleasant and profitable hour.

May dear auld Scotia continue to give to the world men of the William McCormack type, and thus maintain her name and her fame, "wherever Scots may gather."

As an exile son of Newmains, 1 am proud to have known and to have been numbered amongst the personal friends of the author of "Memories O' Hame".

Memories O' Hame.

Respectfully Dedicated to John McNeil, Esq., Denver, Col.

I've been across the sea, John,
  Faur ower the stormy faem,
And spent a happy holiday
  Wi the dear auld folks at hame:
Ay, mony a kindly freen, John,
  I met whin I wis there,
And some I sadly missed, John,
  That's gaen fur ever-mair.

I've been across the sea, John,
  Tae Scotland faur-awa,
I've wandered through her bonnie glens
  And climbed her mountains braw,
And sweetly in the wildwood, John,
  I heard the mavis sing
Aroon' the haunts o' child-hood, John,
  The gledsome notes o' spring.

I've bin tae Bonnie Scotland, John,
    I wish you had bin there,
In a' my pleasant rambles, John,
    And kindred joys tae share.
I saw the heather blooming, John,
    The gowan on the lea,
Amangst the fragrant clover, John,
    I marked the busy bee.

I saw the auld kirk-yaird, John,
    Whaur sleep the village deid,
And mony a weal-kent name, John,
    Upon the stanes I read.
And the auld kirk-ivy-clad, John,
    And the sexton auld and gray,
And the skule-hoose by the green, John,
    Whaur the happy bairnies play.

I've bin tae Bonnie Scotland, John,
    There's music in the name,
Recain' sunny memories, John,
    O' freenship, love and hame,
And cauld maun be the loon, John,
    Wha disna thrill wi pride,
To hear o' "Bonnie Doon", John,
    The Devon, Tweed and Clyde.

I grant this land is fair, John,
    Wi blue ethereal skies,
And rich in treasures rare, John,
    That eager mortals prize.
But, ah! it lacks a charm, John,
    We feel, but canna name,
That mak's oor boosoms warm, John,
    When'er we think o' hame.

Ailie's Awa.

It wis in th' autumn o' th' year
    Ay, weal a' mind th' day—
Th' leaves an' floers wur turnin' sere
    An' hast'nin' tae decay.
Th' hills wur wrapt in hazy hood
    An' mantled owre wi snaw,
A' nature seemed in dowie mood
    Whin Ailie gaed awa.

Faur across th' broad an' furrowed deep
    Oor Ailie she hes gane,
And (a secret a maybe should keep)
    She'll no be back again.
O thou wha guides the surging billow,
    An' th' wee bit sparrow's fa;
Aye gaird her peaceful pillow,
    Oor Ailie that's awa.

Oor Ailie wis a winsome hizzie,
  As rosy as th' dawn,
Wi nimble fingers ever busy,
  As graceful as a fawn.
Hoo sair we miss her in the mornin'
  As weal's at gloamin' fa!
Ne'er tae our hame again returnin',
  Oor Ailie is awa.

Sae noo oor mountain hame is dreary
  Withoot oor Ailie's smile;
Hoo much we miss her sang sae cheery
  Lichtin' our daily toil!
A' things gang wrang aboot th' hoose,
  There's naething richt ava;
E'en oor auld cat is no sae croose
  Since Ailie gaed awa.

In th' shady dell aboot oor cot,
  Whaur rins th' burnie clear;
Aye sendin' oot its plaintive note
  Tae reach ma list'nin' ear.
Whin shin' th' balmy braith o' spring,
  Back tae fu' life 'll ca
Th' floers tae bloom, th' birds tae sing
  But Ailie, she's awa.

Th' Wee While We're Here.

As we journey thro' this world,
   O' bustle, din an' strife;
Let us vie wi ane anither,
   Tae leeve an honest life.
Fur life at maist is but a span,.
   And daith is aye sae near,
Sae let us dae whit guid we can
   Th' wee while that we're here.

We've a' oor faults an' failin's,
   We're deeply steep'd in sin;
Tho' oftentimes oor ootward mask
   Conceals the guilt within.
Then let us throw the mask aside,
   Be upricht an' sincere;
An' dae as muckle guid's we can
   Th' wee while that we're here.

Th' floers adorned n simmer's bloom
　　Hae sune tae fade an' dee
Sae we're fast hast'nin' tae th' tomb,
　　Whaur we'll forgotten be.
But at th' jidgemint sate o' heav'n
　　Our speerits maun appear,
Tae answer fur th' deeds we've dune
　　Th' wee while we've bin here.

Be ready aye wi cheery hert
　　Tae help a' brither on;
There's joy indeed in heav'n abin
　　Whin kindly deeds are dune;
An' whin at last it comes oor turn
　　Tae leave this earthly sphere,
We'll never rue whit guid we've dune
　　Th' wee while we've bin here.

My Village Hame *

O, weel dae a' mind o' ma village hame,
   In fancy a' see it noo—
As it used tae be in ma boyhood days
   E'er care had furrowed ma broo,
A' can hear the tones o' ma mithers
       voice,
   Singin' sae sweet an' low,
The sangs that she sang whin 'we wur
       weans
   By the fireside long ago,

Ma village hame! ma village hame!
   Whit mem'ries roon thee cling—
O' happy days a' ve spent in thee,
   In youth's bright joyous Spring.
O' brithers an' sister's dear
   A' widely scattered noo—
O' merry pranks in skule-lad days,
   Wi comrades leal an' true.

Th' wee cot-hoose aside the burn
    Altho' th' rooms wur sma—
Th' kindly herts that leev-d within
    A welcome had fur a';
Sweet haunts o' happy, youthfu' days
    O' innocence an' glee;.
Thy verdant banks an' bonnie braes
    Wull aye be dear tae me.

---

* The "Village Hame" here referred to is Bonkle a quiet rural village on the banks of the Calder in Cambusnethen Parish, Lanarkshire, Scotland.

My Native Land

A 've often heard o' ither lands,
Faur, faur ayont th' sea,
Whaur nature wi a lavish haund
   Bestows her favours free,
Whaur frits an' flooers an' myrtle bow'rs
   In rich profusion grow,
Wi' lofty mountains tow'ring high
   An' fertile plains below.

Ma native land tho' rugged-wild,
Has still its charms for me
That foreign lands wi a' thair wealth
   An' beauties canna gie.
Its hills an' dells; its mairs an' fells,
Its glens an' birken shaws,
Are hallowed scenes, whaur martys true
   Have died for freedoms cause.

The exile from his native land,
   A home still finds in thee,
And under Britain's noble sway
   The down-trod slave is free.
We own no despot tryant's power,
   We fear no braggart knave,
For Justice, Truth and Mercy rule
   Where British banners wave.

To my worthy friend Alexander Sneddon, Esq., of Engleville, Colorado, lately returned from a visit to Scotland

Just now I have an hour to spare,
    So down I sit to write you—
And let me tell you on the square,
    I never meant to slight you.
But better late than ne'er do weal
    I've heard at Kirk and Weddin',
The words o' mony an honest chiel,
    Believe me, Sandy Sneddon.

No doubt we shirk our duty whiles,
    And say there's time tomorrow,
But when we heed the tempter's wiles
    He's sure to bring us sorrow.
Procrastination is a thief
    The "guid book" I have read in,
And time flies fast, and life is brief,
    Believe me Sandy Sneddon.

But now, dear friend you must not think,
  I mean to write a sermon,
Or idly to make words clink—
  In English, French or German,
O' no, that's scarcely in the line
  That I was born and bred in;
I ne'er could boast of gifts divine
  Believe me, Sandy Sneddon.

I'd really like to see you noo,
  And hear the news "frae Scottland,"
'Bout what ye saw, and what was new
  Wha met ye at the boat-land?
And did ye gang to Embro 'town
  Or cross the Mair to redden'?---
To see 't again I'd gie a croon,
  Believe me, Sandy Sneddon.

And did ye walk by old Kinniel
  By Lilburns ghost yet haunted?
Or where Michael Scott once told "ye deil"
  Ane Brygge Meikle wanted?
Or did ye look on Falkirk hearth
  Where Patriot Wallace led on
A gallant band to glorious death?
  Believe me Sandy Sneddon.

My best regards to wife and bairn,
    (How is the little lady?)
With much regret indeed, I learn
    That seldom yet comes pay-day;
The masters hardly seem to care
    How? when? or what? we're fed on,
As long's they get the lion's share---
    Believe me Sandy Sneddon.

Accept this, friend of genuine worth,
    Fraternally I greet you,
And in Boness, beside the Forth
    Wha kens? I yet may meet you,
And if a policeman dare frown
    On him we'll put a "head on."
For by my faith we'll paint the town,
    Believe me Sandy Sneddon,

Parted

Beneath the greenwood tree they stood,
  Where fretted shadows thickly fell,
And there he tries to muster strength---
  To speak his words of sad farewell,
Before he quit these scenes beloved
  To battle with an angry sea,
He said; "I tell thee once again,
  I love but thee! I love but thee!"
The dangers haunt the mighty deep,
  Oh, let not grief thy bosom fret:
Thy love shall bear me safe through all,
  More safe than fairy amulet.
Ere twenty moons have lit the heavens,
  By thy dear side again I'll be
Once more to whisper in thine ear,
  "I love but thee! I love but thee!"
'Till then shall fancy conjure up
  Thy winsome face to light mine eyes,
And in my every dream thou'lt shine

My guiding star of cloudless skies.
Till then, while seasons come and go
    And scenes remote from thee I see,
My heart shall pulse, but one refrain,
    "I love but thee!   I love but thee!"
"He loves but me," she fondly cries
    And seeks to calm his rising fears,
The love-light sparkles in her eyes
    Dim with the flow of happy tears,
And as she treads her homeward path,
    The whisper bounds from tree to tree,
"He loves but me!   He loves but me!"
Upon a lonely wave-beat abore,
    Her watch, a weeping maiden keeps
And scans wild-eyed the waters cold
    Where deep her sailor-lover sleeps;
While far above his lowly head
    The careless breezes whistle free,
"He will; He will come back she moans,
    He loves but me !He loves but me'

Auld Mamie

Auld Mamie puir body, leav'd doon
    in the dell
    Naebody leev'd near her, so she wis a'
        by her sel',
Th' folk o' th' clachin; wur feart o' their
    life,
    For thae a' thocht that Mamie wis a
        weirdy auld wife.
    Th' gossips a' cad' auld Mamie a
        witch,
An' said 'twas th' deil that had made
    her sae rich,
    Efter nicht they wur feart tae gang
        doon by th' dell
In case she'd cast over them some ill-
    omened spell,

But Mamie, auld budy put her trust aye
    in God,
  As she sat by th' fire in her lonely
    abode,
Or kneeled doon and prayed on her ain
    hearthstane,
  Ay, God wis aye wi her, she wis
    never alane.

Adieu My Love *

Adieu My Love! stern fortune's frown
    Compels us now to sever ;
But tho' afar from thee I roam,
    Forget thee—I will never.
Each sacred vow so fondly pledged,
    Within my breast I'll cherish,
Yes, I to thee will faithful be
    'Till life itself shall perish

Adieu my love! when far from thee
    Beyond the rolling billow,
My thought by day thou still shalt be,
    In dreams thou'lt halt my pillow
Cheer up my love, come dry thy tears
    Tho' now we part in sorrow ;
The fickle jade that frowns today,
    May brightly smile tomorrow.

* Written while contemplating going abroad.

Scotia's Darling Bard

Written for a Burn's celebration held at Florence, Colorado, on January 25th, 1895

Ye powers that rule the fates of men,
    My wanderin, wits restore me,
To shape my thoughts and guide my pen
    I humbly do implore ye.
To lofty strains I ne'er aspire,
    But jist some hamely jingle—
Gi'e me ae spark o' nature's fire
    That mak's the hert-strings tingle.

"The 25th" again returns
    Auld time my mem'ry joggin'
The natal-day of Scotland's Burns,
    Oor ain immortol Robin;
And here beside the Arkansaw
    We've met to sound the praises
Of him who sweetly sings of a'
    The dear familiar places.

The bonnie lassies—bless them a
    He sweetly sung aboot them
And wisely held by nature's law
    The world would end withoot them.
But if he saw them noo, he'd stare,
    With wonder on his features,
To see them ride a wheel and wear—
    He'd hardly ken the creatures.

The inmost passions of the heart,
    He pictured forth with feeling,
And grace beyond the reach of art,
    The heart-to-heart appealing;
And surely when we love him best
    'Tis when he climbs "Parnassus",
And sweetly sings 'bove a' th' rest
    Of Scotland's bonnie lassies.

Hypocrisy he aye abhorred,
    And uncannily exposed it;
But friendship firm and fast bestowed
    Whereever he reposed it;
It mattered not for humble lot,
    When genuine worth he found it,
With stamp of genius burning hot
    He cast a halo around it.

In every land beneath the Sun,
　　Whereever Scotsmen mingle:
Mid scenes of death where fields are won'
　　Or round the cheerful ingle;
His strains have nerved the soldiers arm
　　To noble deeds of daring,
And lent to noble youth a charm
　　Unbounded and unsparing

The stalwart ploughman on the lee—
　　The rosy milkmaid cheery,
The sailor boy far out at sea,
　　On midnight watch so dreary;
Tho' born to heritage of toil,
　　What e'er may be denied us
We glory in our native soil
　　And the songs that Burns has gi'en us

The Lass I Met at Penty

Air—"THE RIGS O' BARLEY"

I hae been oot at mony o' spree,
   Wi comrades blythe an' canti o'
But by faur the happiest nicht tae me
   Wis that happy nicht at Penty o'
      CHORUS
That happy nicht, that happy nicht,
   That happy nicht at Penty o',
The win may blaw, an the rain may fa'
   But we'll aye ca' back at Penty o'.

I hae bin in th' gaudy ha—
   I hae seen lassies plenty o',
But there's nane tae me, seems hauf
    sae fair,
   As the lass I met at Penty o'.
   Chorus—That happy nicht etc.

She was a merry modest queen
    Her face was sweet an' dainty o',
A brawer lass there cud na be
    Than th' lass I met at Penty o'.
        Chorus ---That happy nicht etc

If I had wealth at my command
    If I had thoosan's twenty o'
I wid gie them a' fur th' hert and haund,
    O' th' lass that I met at Penty o',
        Chorus --- That happy nicht etc.

But fortune tae me's no sae kind
    Sae I maun be contented o',
But still that happy nicht I'll mind,
    And the lass that I met at Penty o'.
That happy nicht, that happy nicht
    That happy nicht at Penty o'
The win may blaw an' th' rain may fa'
    But we'll aye ca' back at Penty o'.

Auld Scotland

I canna boast o' college lear,
   I ken nae rules o' grammar;
And pen and ink I haundle queer,
   Compared wi file and hammer
But whiles I'm fain tae tune ma lyre
   And sing auld Scotland's praise
Tho' lacking in poetic fire,
   And couched in hamely phrase

Oh, Scotland! dear auld Scotland!
   Faur owre th' stormy deep;
The land whaur first I saw th' licht
   And whaur ma kindred sleep:
Nae ither land surpasses
   The land o' hill and glen,
Fur bonnie, winsome lassies
   And gallant-herted men.

Oh, Scotland! dear auld Scotland!
  The land I love so well,
Where the purple, bloomin' heather
    grows,
  And the noddin' sweet blue - bell ;
The hawthorne white, the yellow broom,
  And th' bonnie rowan tree,
They load the breeze wi sweet perfume
  That wafts frae sea to sea.

Hail! Scotland! grand auld Scotland!
  The land o' Wallace brave,
Who for his country and her cause
  His life so nobly gave :
On many a field o' carnage
  In Scotland's darkest hour
He bore her flag untarnished,
  Defying Edward's power.

Oh! Scotland, glorious Scotland,
  Where "Guide King Robert" rang
The theme o' martial story,
  And many a minstrel's sang :
He quelled the proud invader
  Who dared our rights to spurn,
And Scotland free, he made her
  The Bruce of Bannockburn.

Oh! Scotland, leal auld Scotland,
  Whaur the buirdly thistle waves,
And the mairland breezes murmur
  Owre the martyrs lonely graves;
Whom Heaven's Lord on High, lent
  The kindly mist to shroud,
When the voice of man was silent
  And the voice of blood was loud.

Oh! dear auld mither, Scotland,
  Thy sons and daughters fair,
In every clime, in prose and rhyme
  Belaud thy beauties rare;
Across the trackless ocean
  A weary hert oft turns
To thee with warm devotion,
  The land of Scott and Burns.

Oh, Robbie, Burns! Oh, Robbie Burns!
  'Tis much indeed we owe thee,
And vain regret each true heart mourns,
  The world too late did know thee;
But such too oft is genius' fate,
  In every age and nation—
In life to meet with scorn and hate
  When dead—with adulation

Ailie wi th' Gowden Hair

Ailie wi th' gowden hair,
   Winsome Ailie; witchin' Ailie;
Wis a lassie e'er sae fair
   In a' th' world afore?
Wistfu e'en o' bonnie blue,
   Rosy cheek and snaw-white broo,
Queen ower a' oor herts are you,
   And humbly we adore thee.

Ailie has a form divine,
   Modest Ailie; graceful Ailie;
Prood am a' tae ca' her mine
   And boo tae her dominion:
Sweet as gowans on th' lee,
   Happy herted, blythe and free,
Merry as a lark can be,
   That soars on airy pinions,

Ailie in the days tae come
    Blythesome Ailie ; lithsome Ailie ;
Happy may'st thou be with one
    Tae cherish thee and love thee ;
Tae shelter thee from every blast ,
    And love thee fondly tae th' last ,
And when th' storms o' life are past
    Be true as Heaven above thee .

Pairtin' at th' Brimilaw

Ae darksome morn, wi tearfu'e'e
   I saw ma laddie sail awa'—
And whin we pairted on th' quay
   I thocht ma hert wid brek in twa.
Oh! hard I tried ma grief tae hide
   But aye th' bitter tear wid fa-
And life o' licht and joy seemed deid,
   Whin pairtin' at the Brimilaw.

He whispered words o' hope tae me
   He vow'd he wid come back again,
And tho' divided by the sea
   His hert wid aye be a' ma ain;
The busy crood we stood amang,
   I scarcely heard, I scarcely saw,
But, ah! it was a bitter pang---
   That pairtin' at th' Brimilaw.

At nicht whin a' is hushed in sleep,
  Again I see him in ma dreams,
And haun tae haun we sclim th' steep
  Or rove thro' glens by crystal streams
Again I hear his whispered vows —
  I winner if he minds them a' —
I ne'er can think th' laddie fause —
  That left me at th' Brimilaw

Thae tell me that I'm fadin' noo —
  Ma raven hair is tinged wi' gray
And furrowed lines across ma brow
  Are signs o' care and youth's decay:
But still within ma hert o' herts.
  Wi fondest mem'ries I reca' —
Th' blissful boors I've spent wi him
  That left me at th' Brimilaw.

Ah ! weary years hae passed since then
  Thro' simmer's heat and winter's snaw
But whin ma laddie comes again,
  I'll meet him at th' Brimilaw.
Ye winds that sweep across th' main,
  In gently zephers saftly blaw,
And bring th' laddie back again —
  That left me at th' Brimilaw.

Faur ower yon wild, wide western plains,
    That in th' distance meet th' skies,
Bleached by th' wanton winds and rains
    His mould'ring form unburied lies,
By savage Indians cruelly slain,
    Life, love and hope are endit a'
On earth we meet nae mair again—
    Thae pairted at th' Brimilaw.

My Teenie was the Fairest

I met her in th' glen one day,
    When summer flowers were blooming,
And little birdies blythe and gay
    Their merry pipes were tuning:
Amongst the fragrance of th' hay
    And lovely flowers the fairest.
I vow'd with pride that Summer day
    My Teenie was the fairest.

I met her in th' glen one day
    When all breathed joy and gladness,
And winter's storms seemed far away,
    No touch of care and sadness;
Dame nature don'd her freshest green,
    By sparkling streams the clearest,
And lovliest of that lovely scene,
    My Teenie was the rarest.

I met her in th' glen one day,
    When summer flowers were fading,
'Midst autumn tints of brown and gray
    And fair fields harvest-laden.
Oh! were I doomed to exile drear
    On earth's bleak spot, the barest,
Her image still my heart would cheer--
    My Teenie is the fairest.

What Could I Do?

What could I do, but love her?
   The brightest, sweetest flower;
The theme of all my fancies,
   Thro' many a lonesome hour:
Her smiles of sunny gladness,
   Her gentle, graceful mien,
Dispelling care and sadness,
   Creation's fairest queen.

What could I do, but love her?
   So trusting, fond and true.
The highest earthly rapture
   My young heart ever knew;
Tho' distance may divide us
   And years may pass away,
The love I bear my darling
   Will last for aye and aye.

The Days are Creepin' In

The corn is ripenin' on th' fields,
   The leaves are turnin' broon,
The simmer flooers are fadin' noo
   And sadly droopin' doon,
I sit ootside th' door at e'en,
   Efter ma sair day's wark is dune,
And watch th' shades o' gloamin' fa',—
   The days are creepin' in.

I loe th' gledsome simmer days,
   Sae sunny and sae long,
On nature's beauties then tae gaze
   And roam her sweets amang;
I hail wi joy th' birds and flooers,
   Sweet gifts frae Heaven abune,
But dowie dreed th' winter's storms
   Whin days are creepin' in

The year is fast declinin',
  The simmer noo is gane,
And could I like the swallow flee
  I'd follow in its train :
Cauld winter wi its bitter blasts
  Wull be upon us sune,
The rustlin' breezes whisper—
  The days are creepin' in.

The storms o' life we canna shun
  Tho' fierce and wild thae be,
And as tae hoo and whan thae'll come
  'Tis hid frae you and me :
Kind providence in mercy
  O' that hes kept us blin'
We sudna fret or murmur,
  Oor days are creepin' in,

My Little Sweetheart Nan

'Tis long years syne, yet weel I mine
   When first I met the fairy,
Whose winsome face I love to trace,
   In lines that never vary;
The passing years with hopes and fears,
   Bring age to maid and man,
But still the same to me appears,
   My little sweetheart Nan.

I was a stripling in my teens,
   And she was young and fair,
Then life was bright with fairy dreams
   And " castles in the air ";
No high-born dame with lofty name,
   E'er coyed with jewelled fan,
As this " faire maide " with my heart
     played,
   My little sweetheart Nan.

I was her escort everywhere,
  Her beau, her cavalier ,
At rustic dance, or country fair ,
  Most ardent and sincere ,
That story old, so often told ,
  Since first the world began ,
Yet fresh and new as morning dew ,
  I told to sweetheart Nan.

I went with her to Kirk o' Shotts
  One summer Sabbath day ,
But of the sermon took no notes ,
  I'm most ashamed to say :
I heeded not when parson prayed—
  My conduct you may ban---
I only worshipped this fair maid ,
  My litttle sweetheart Nan .

How fair the woods of Murdostoun ,
  When clad in summer green ,
And bonnie are the flowery howms
  By Calder's winding stream ;
And after then when gloamin' fell
  Ower a' th' pleasant lan'
I roved through Calder's bosky dell ,
  With little sweetheart Nan .

The years hae gane each weel-kent name
    Has still the power to charm ,
As when I used to see her hame
    Around by Swinstie farm ;
And while I sojourn here below
    Thro' life's allottted span ,
My hert will feel a kindly glow
    For little sweetheart Nan .

Calder's Bonnie Glen

Now, gentle spring returns ainee mair,
　　The gowans deck the plain,
The wild birds 'mong the buddin' trees
　　Send forth a joyful strain;
Tae view the charms o' nature
　　Nae sweeter nook I ken,
For fair in ilka feature
　　Is Calder's bonnie glen.

E'en in the deid o' winter
　　A cosy look it wears,
And there in early spring-time
　　The primrose first appears;
Amd there the lover meets his dear,
　　The happy hours tae spen'
Beneath the fragrant hawthorne
　　In Calder's bonnie glen.

'Twas there in childhood's happy days
   Unclouded free frae care,
  pu'd th' brambles and the slaes
   That grow in plenty there;
And tho' I've been in distant lands
   And changes seen since then,
My memory loves tae linger
   In Calder's bonnie glen.

Beside the Calder

Sweet Calder! winding Calder!
  Beside thy woodland stream,
Where shadows play this autumn day,
  I sit alone and dream;
The murmur of thy waters,
  Seems to my listening ears,
Now gay with rippling laughter,
  Now sad with wail of tears.

Sweet Calder! winding Calder!
  A pilgrim at thy shrine,
Here oft I've roved with playmates loved,
  In days of auld lang syne:
Tho' long in lands far distant,
  'Neath glowing western skies,
Fond memory, warm, insistent
  Recalls those youthful ties.

The hazel, birch and tasel'd larch
   Still shades the swimming pool
That once was spanned by Roman arch,
   And oft when free from school
We sported in the water clear ,
   In merry boyish mood ,
And often fled with haste and fear
   From "Keeper" stern and rude .

In glorious days of snmmer
   I've wandered by your side ,
From muirland burn, where you are born
   Until ye join the Clyde,
I've watched your useful duties ,
   In mills and marts of men ,
And lingered with your beauties
   In Westwood's lonely glen .

Sweet Calder ! murmuring Calder !
   Old story-haunted stream ,
Where fairy sprites oft danced o' nichts
   By moonlights mellow gleam;
The water-kelpie whiles was seen ,
   When Lammas floods were high ,
And mingling with the hoolet's scream ,
   Was heard "Old Clootie's" cry .

Long years have passed above me,
  I'm getting gray and old,
Warm hearts that used to love me
  Are in the kirkyard cold:
Their work on earth is over,
  Their spirits passed away
And yet they seem to hover
  Around me here today.

With joy akin to sadness
  These scenes again I view,
Our days of youth and gladness
  Are fleeting, short and few,
The stream flows to the river,
  The river to the sea,
And stream and men forever,
  To vast eternities.

The Auld Kirkyard *

(AN AUTUMN REVERIE)

The autumn winds are sighing
   With sad and mournful sound,
The leaves are thickly lying,
   Upon each grassy mound:
The little robin red-breast,
   Hops lightly o'er the sward,
That wraps the slumbering tenants
   In the auld kirkyard.

Within these silent portals,
   Ah! bitter tears are shed,
By suffering fellow-mortals
   In anguish o'er their dead;
And cherished flowers are tended,
   And monuments are reared
In memory of the dear ones
   In the auld kirkyard.

Tread softly o'er their pillows,
  And speak with reverence low,
Beneath these drooping willows,
  Secure from pain and woe,
The youth, the gentle maiden,
  The grandsire, silver-haired,
In death's long sleep is laid
  In the auld kirkyard.

Here playmates of our childhood,
  Who long since passed away,
And friends of manhood's upper years
  Lie mingling in decay;
And loving hearts that warmly
  Our joys and sorrows shared,
In death's long sleep are laid
  In the auld kirkyard.

No dreams disturb their slumbers
  No angry passions rave,
The flowers that bloom and wither,
  Above the peaceful grave—
Convey the solemn warning,
  We must all be prepared
To lie beside our kindred
  In the auld kirkyard.

My Mither's Spinnin' Wheel

Now busy fancy fills my mind,
　Wi memories o' th' past,
And visions of my youthful days
　Come tae me thick and fast;
And thro' th' mists o' bygane years
　Come scenes remembered weel—
Oor blythe fireside, my faither's chair,
　And mither's spinning wheel.

Wi thrifty haun she span th' 'oo,
　Tae mak' th' hodder gray,
Or checkit-plaid of white and blue—
　She wore fur mony a day.
Auld Scotland's lassies trig and braw
　I wat look unco weel,
When by the ingleside they ca'
　The hummin' spinnin' wheel.

When wintry winds wi surly gusts
   Were blawin' cauld and keen,
Aroond the fire—a merry group—
   We gathered in at e'en;
We heeded-na th' angry blasts,
   Sae happy did we feel
As faither read his paper, while
   My mither turned her wheel.

O, happy days! whin life was young,
   Wi a' the world afore,
We thocht o' but th' pleasures then
   The future held in store:
But stoppin' noo' and lukin' back,
   Thro' life's sair fankled reel,
I min' th' words my mither spak'
   Beside her spinnin' wheel.

But years hae passed since ane and a'
   We left th' auld rooftree,
And some sleep in th' auld kirkyard,
   And some are ower th' sea :
But often whin I lay me doon,
   Ere sleep my e'-lids seal,
I see again my boyhood's hame,
   And hear th' spinnin' wheel.

An Old Man's Address To His Wife*

Come here guid wife' jist sit ye doon,
   And rest yirsel' a while,
I like tae hear yir kindly words,
   And see yer pleasant smile;
It makes the bygane days o' youth
   Rise up afore ma view;
We've seen the morn o' life, dear Jean,
'Tis gloamin' wi us noo.

We've had oor cares and sorrows Jean
   As ilka ane maun hae,
An mony a weary struggle Jean,
   Tae sclim life's slippery brae,
A helpmate still in time o' need,
   Ye aye wis leal and true,
We've seen th' morn o' life, dear Jean,
   'Tis gloamin' wi us now.

Oor sons and dochters hae grown up,
   And left us ane by ane,
That little grand-bairn on yir knee,
   We fondly ca' "oor ain",
In years tae come if she be spared,
   She'll often think o' you:
We've seen the morn of life, dear Jean
   'Tis gloamin' wi us noo.

The spring o' life has langsyne past,
   And gane is simmer's bloom,
Sere autumn's slippin unco fast,
   And near is winter's gloom.
O' may we in that better land,
   Wauken tae life anew;
We've seen th' morn o' life, dear Jean,
   'Tis gloamin' wi us noo.

The Auld Hoose at Hame

There are scenes in our lives that we
    love to remember
  (And others perhaps that we fain
    would forget)
Of the loves o' our youth, sae fond,
    true and tender,
  That awakens a thrill in our fond
    memories yet,
Ah! how dear to the hearts are the
    haunts of our childhood,
  Tho' distant afar o'er the wide roll-
    ing main,
Recalling gay rambles by stream, glen
    and wildwood,
  And the warm hearts that loved in
    the auld hoose at hame.

By yon greenwood glade, where the
    Calder rins clearly,
    And the notes of the cuckoo are first
       heard in spring;
Where the crawflowers and primrose
    bloom sweetly and early,
    And the blackbird and mavis make
       the wood echoes ring,
There stands a wee hoosie, embower'd
    'midst the flowers,
    And the sweet honey-suckle keeks in at
       the pane,
    And there, when a laddie, I've spent
       happy hours,
By Calder's green banks, near the auld
    hoose at hame.

Ah! bright is the dawning of life's early
    morning,
    When licht is the heart that kens
       nocht o' care,
But love casts it glamour in spite o' the
    warning,
    That beauty alas! often blooms to
       ensnare;

Still deep in my bosom, I yet fondly
  cherish,
  The memory of one who awoke the
  soft flame,
And never till life and memory shall per-
  ish
  Can I forget her, or the auld hoose
  at hame.

In the lang days o' simmer, when the
  blue bells and heather,
  Were blooming sae bonnie ower
  mountain and mair,
When wee thochtless laddies hoo often
  th' geither,
  We've chased the wild bee and the
  butter-fly there.
Oh! ainee happy days, that hae van-
  ished forever
  My playmates of childhood, whaur
  hae they a' gane?
Ah! mony hae crossed ower the dark,
  silent river,
  And ithers are faur frae the auld
  hoose at hame.

Oh! Bonkle, dear village, how often I
ponder
On the sweet sylvan scenes, I once
knew so well,
And tho' in a strange land, far distant I
wander,
I see them again under fancy's bright
spell;
The roses still bloom in the garden sae
fair,
The trim hawthorn hedges yet bordee
the lane,
But, ah! there is ane that I'll never ser
mair,
The licht and the love o' the auld
hoose at hame.

An Emigrant's Sigts

Written on board the steamer "Pavonia" of the Cunard
line during the voyage from Liverpool to Boston,
September 17th to September 28th, 1891.

Dear land of my father's thou'rt fading
    from sight,
    As darkness enshrouds the wild
    main,
The morning will scatter the shades of
    the night,
    But never may I see thee again.
Dear land of my sires! the land of my
    birth,
    The home of the brave and the free ;
Wherever I wander o,er all the wide
    earth
    My heart will beat warmly for thee.

The dark heather waves o'er the mount-
    ain and moor,

And thy streams as they flow to the
    sea
Are singing a dirge for the heroes of
    yore—
Who died that our land might be free;
O, where is the land that with thee can
    compare
    In song, or in soul-stirring story!
Enshrined in the hearts of thy sons ev-
    erywhere,
    Are the words of undying glory.

Farewell, thou dear land! tho' never
    again
    My feet shall trample thy heather;
Farewell each green mountain, and val-
    ley and plain !
    Rare beauties all clustered together.
Dear land of my sires! the land of my
    birth,
    The home of the brave and the free,
Wherever I wander o'er all the wide
    earth
    My heart will beat warmly for thee.

Robert Burns

Read by the Author at a Burns' Anniversary in Walsenberg, Colorado, January 25th, 1894.

This night in many a distant clime
    Auld Scotland's sons have met with
      pride,
In honour of her ploughman bard
    Whose fame rings thro' the world-wide
Wher'er you meet the wand'ring Scot,
    Wher'er is heard the doric tongue,
In lordly hall, or humble cot,
    Are heard the songs that Robin sung.

He sang the "Lad was born in Kyle,
    A cantie lit aboot himsel',
His partner in the harvest toil
    When but a lad, his "Handsome Nell";
His "Mary Dear" who soundly sleeps,
    Beside the Clyde in Ceenock toon;

His "Darling Jean", the "Banks of Ayr",
  "Sweet Ballochmyle" and "Bonnie
    Doon".

With master hand he touched the lyre,
  And sweet and clear his wood-notes
wild,
Came throbbing, trembling at the touch,
  Of nature's bard, her darling child.
Hark! how he woos in tender strains,
  And now with passions "wild and
    strong",
And country maids and rustic swains,
  Are framed in never-dying song.

We mark him toiling at the plough,
  With glowing eyes and heart elate,
Or, musing perchance with pensive brow,
  On "Daisy" crushed, or "Mousie's"
    fate:
For weary cattle in the stall,
  His tender heart can pity feel,
Extended to Creation all
  He pities e'en the very "kiel"

We see him in the festive ha'—
    The guest of lords and ladies gay,
With "aye a hert aboon them a'
    Tho' clad in home-spun hodder grey;
Let us a' toast his memory here,
    While yearly as the day returns
His name to mankind grows more dear,
    Auld Scotland's Bard-Immortal Burns

The Engineer

Read by the author before a meeting of the
Master Mechanics' Club, of Cripple Creek Dis-
trict, Colorado, in February, 1900.

My theme is not a "gallant knight"
   Nor gentle "ladye faire";
It is no romance that I would write
   Your fancy to ensnare;
But musing on the "passing show"
   I start my rhyming gear,
To sing the praises of one you know,
   The humble engineer.

Of late we've read and heard about
   The man behind the gun,
Of how he "knocked the Spaniard out
   And glorious victory won";
A tribute to his worth we pay
   With many a rousing cheer
But seldom have a word to say
   About the engineer.

When stormy winds at sea prevail,
   Yon steamship, tempest-tossed,
Has weathered out the fearful gale,
   And safely reached the coast;
The passenger, with tongue and pen
   And costly souvenir,
All think about the captain then,
   But where's the engineer?

O'er mountain pass, thro' tunnel black,
   The iron horse swiftly flies,
And ever brooding o'er the track,
   Death lurks in awful guise;
And ever looking out ahead,
   To mark the "white light" clear,
The "cautious green" or "danger red"
   You'll find the engineer.

The miner steps upon the cage,
   Or on the bucket clings,
In perilous labour to engage,
   That wealth and comfort brings;
Of all the men who "handle steam"
   The one who has no peer,
"Par excellence," "creme de la creme"
   Is the hoisting engineer.

There are heroes in the ranks of peace
　　As well's the ranks of war,
Who battle with life's troubled seas,
　　And suffer wound and scar;
And many a noble deed is done
　　Of which we never hear,
And many a brilliant victory won
　　By the humble engineer.

The Miner

Who toils in caverns dark and drear,
Where rays of sunshine never cheer,
Where death and danger's ever near?
                The Miner.

Who toils beset with many a foe,
'Midst treach'rous gas that lurks below,
And bursting water's dreadful flow?
                The Miner.

In weary toil, day after day,
Whilst health and vigour soon decay,
Ah! hard his lot and scant his pay,
                The Miner.

Far down beneath the verdant fields,
Where mother earth her treasure yields,
With weary arms his pick he wields,
                The Miner.

His trade supports our commerce free,
And spreads our wealth o'er land and sea,
Ah! much indeed we owe to thee,
                    Poor Miner.

Then let us prize the miner's skill,
And bear him friendship and goodwill,
Remember, he's our brother still,
                    The Miner.

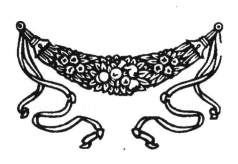

Danny McLaren

Success and good health to you, Danny McLaren,
And honours and wealth to you, Danny McLaren,
By the top of Pike's Peak, and that's mighty tall
       swearin',
Ye ken whaur tae seek, man, Danny McLaren.

Ye're a real mining expert, Danny McLaren,
Sae ye're na cheeky upstart, Danny McLaren,
The camp they had killed it as deid as a herrin',
But wi' fresh life ye've filled it, Danny McLaren.

'Twixt knockers and knockers, Danny McLaren,
They've knocked the life oot the stocks, Danny
      McLaren,
Till hunger and ruin in our faces are starin',
And anarchy brewin', man, Danny McLaren.

We hivna heard the last frae ye, Danny McLaren,
We will yet get a blast frae ye, Danny McLaren,
Ye're pipes are your ain and dinna be sparin',
Sae strike up again, man, Danny McLaren.

The Man Who Hunts a Job

The sun is shining bright today,
   The skies are blue and clear,
The mountains that are far away
   Appear to be quite near;
Dame Nature wears a smiling face
   (Tho' somewhat scanty robe),
A grateful and redeeming grace
   To the man who hunts a job.

He suffers many a heart-ache
   When he asks for "daily bread";
He gets many an answer—arctic,
   And sometimes a stone instead.
While "clothed in brief authority,"
   He meets with many a snob
Who smiles with sneeriority
   On the man who hunts a job.

When fiercely drives the wintry blast,
  And deep the drifting snow,
When wanderings of the day are past,
  How cheerful is the glow
Of evening fire, while merrily steams
  The kettle on the hob,
Then bright the hopes and waking dreams
  Of the man who hunts a job.

I envy not the sordid rich
  With all their selfish cares,
Whose lives are set at market pitch—
  Valued by stocks and shares.
A kindly heart is a noble chart,
  There's joy in every throb,
The greatest master of his art
  May sometimes hunt a job.

Johnnie Walters

To my dear friend, Joseph Patterson,
Florence, Colorado

Dear Joe, I somehow fear you'll think
    I'm rather long in writing,
And freely own the task I shrink
    When I have no delight in.
Your slightest wishes I'll attend,
    Ne'er count me, 'mong defaulters,
Besides, I'm pleased, my worthy friend,
    To hear of Johnnie Walters.

If I had but the painter's art,
    Divinely I'd portray him,
The beaming eye, when kindly heart
    With tender passions sway him;
Or were I gifted with the muse
    That neither fails nor falters,
My heaven-born gifts I'd gladly use
    In praise of Johnnie Walters.

For drinking bouts and rabble routs
    I have a great abhorrence,
But for Soda Springs and other things
    I'll own "I'm stuck on Florence";
And when I go to that fair town,
    I'll seek the house that shelters,
And o'er a brew, sweet joys renew,
    With you and Johnnie Walters.

And mind ye, Joe, and tell him so,
    My compliments I send him,
A guid New Year, may health and cheer
    Through all his life attend him;
And who in this see aught amiss
    I wish their necks in halters,
For I'll maintain I'd like again
    To meet with Johnnie Walters.

And further yet, pray don't forget,
    Remember me to Glasson
And his good wife—upon my life,
    I wish my pen would pass on
O'er friendly names and comely dames
    Like wayward steed it falters,
So I'll conclude my rhyming mood
    With love to Johnnie Walters.

John McNeil, M. E.

To John McNeil, M. E., Denver, Col.

My dear friend, John, with right good will
  I've read your kindly letter,
The more you run your writing mill
  It seems to work the better.
From mine reports, concise and terse,
  It turns with little friction
To shape a smoothly flowing verse,
  And whiles—a playing fiction.

For truth, no "man of men" am I,
  A very common mortal—
The door of fame, were I to try,
  I'd never reach the portal;
Tho' once a wild dream filled my mind
  To be "Engineer Professor"—
But now for means to raise the wind
  I run an Air Compressor.

But, pardon, John, I'm well content,
   I've health and all my senses—
I'm able aye to meet the rent
   And other small expenses;
The little sum that Teenie saves
   (It's bankit wi' "my uncle")
May help us canny to our graves—
   Or a cottage hame in Bonkle.

But, John, your skill is in demand,
   Profoundly scientific—
From Yukon to the Rio Grande,
   Atlantic to Pacific.
You read the rocks like printed page
   With knowledge sound, veracious,
From lower Paleozoic age—
   To upper Cretaceous.

You've travelled many "weary miles"
   Since last we saw each other,
From far northwest to British Isles,
   From sage-brush to the heather;
You've trod the busy haunts of men—
   And crossed o'er lofty mountains,
You've roved thro' lonely Highland glen
   By clear perennial fountains.

I'm pleased to hear you've rugged health,
  And wish you aye full share o't,
Forbye a modicum of wealth
  And judgment to take care o't;
But words of caution should be few
  From one whose barque has drifted,
Tho' even with a steady crew
  The cargo whiles gets shifted.

Mention us to the good, old man,
  With kindliest heart-felt wishes,
Who, tho' beyond the allotted span.
  Still bravely meet's life's issues
A heavy blow was Ronald's loss
  To him and sister Nellie;
Lord, strengthen them to bear their cross,
  And lead them through the valley.

I'm truly sorry, John, to hear
  Your dear wife is so poorly,
But hope for words of better cheer,
  Her illness lingers drearily;
Our compliments to her and you
  Are cordially extended,
And may our friendship, leal and true,
  By death alone be ended.

P. S.—I know you're pressed with business cares
  "Too numerous to mention,"
That whiles ev'n some of "Teddy's Bears"
  Demand your close attention;
But write me, John, when e'er you've time
  (Let typist think we're "silly"),
Please don't remark the ready rhyme,
  That last word is for "Willie."

The Udston Mine Disaster

To the Brave Rescuers

What tho' no medal decks your breast
   To tell of deeds you've done,
Nor courtly bards in fulsome strain
   Your victories have sung;
A nobler band with hearts more brave
   Ne'er stood in battle line,
Than ye who risked your lives to save
   In Udston's fatal mine.

When up the shaft with lurid glare
   The gas flames quickly spread
And fancy pictured with despair
   The dying and the dead;
No craven cowards 'mongst you then,
   Tho' well the risks you knew;
You thought but of your fellow men
   And hastened to rescue.

Then tho' no medals deck your breasts,
  No laurel wreaths your brow,
You still have that which serves you best,
  Which kings can ne'er bestow;
The willing hands, the dauntless heart,
  The sense of duty done,
And all the praise the world may give,
  'Twas surely nobly won.

To a Comrade in America

To William Cairns, who left the Law, in the
Parish of Carluke, for America, in 1866.

Aince mair, dear Wull, wi' joyfu' hert,
   I've read yir letter thro',
And prood I am tae see thereby
   That you, and those ye loo—
In yir hame across the sea,
   Are a' sae guid and healthy,
Ma earnest prayer for ye a'
   Is, that ye may shin be wealthy.

It's true, dear Wull, the auld place noo,
   I think, ye'd haurdly ken;
The lauchin' bairnies o' your day,
   Are noo oor wives and men;
Ithers hae gaun tae distant lands
   Like you, tae push abeid,
Ithers lie in the auld Kirkyaird,
   Amongst oor saintly deid.

Wull, often in ma summer walks,
    I dauner tae Lawhaull;
Whit mem'ries then o' ither days
    As I gang by the mull;
Alas, it's a' in ruins noo,
    The dam's a' broken doon,
The muckle wheel grown over wi' weeds
    Nae mair gangs merr'ly roon.

The muller, tae, ye speak o' him—
    Ye mind auld Tam Muirheid,
Weel, prood am I tae tell ye, Wull,
    That aul Tam isna deid;
He's leevin' yet and workin' tae,
    Tho' fast gaun doon the hull,
Let's houp it'll be mony a day
    Ere he is like the mull.

Ye min tae, Wull, aboon the Gill
    The place we used tae sit
And lauch at ither's stories, till
    Oor sides wur like tae split.
And hoo we made the echoes ring
    And scared the birds away,
As in mimic strife we tried tae push
    Ilk ither doon the brae.

And dae ye mind white strolls we had
  O'er mountain, moss and mair,
Whit plans we laid fur efter life,
  Whit castles in the air?
Alas, thae a' hae vanish't noo
  And left the stern and true,
But unco glad I am, dear frien',
  That there's nae change in you.

Ye tell me o' yir Prairie hame,
  Nae doot it's wrondrous fair,
But still I fear wi a' its wealth,
  Ye'll miss the heather sair;
For tho' at hame he's sairly tried,
  Beset wi mony ills,
A Scotsman never can forget
  His native heather hills.

Then aince again ma cronnie dear,
  I wish ye ever weel,
May strength be garnted tae ye aye
  The hull o' life tae speil.
And if tae Scotland ye return
  Tae view her beauties fair,
A herty welcome ye wull get,
  Frae your auld cronnie there.

I Wonder Wha' I'll Meet There

'Tis a maiter I've often pondered o'er,
   And wondered mony a time,
When aboot tae sail fur a foreign shore,
   Or tae veesit a distant clime;
In leavin' the freens and scenes o' lang syne,
   I hae aye felt a pang that wis sair,
But the query that oftenest comes tae ma min'
   Is—I winner wha I'll meet there?

Not long ago, down to Old Mexico,
   On a mission I was sent;
'Tis a land of romance, of hazard and chance,
   Of mosquitoes, and strife, and torment;
In political dreams, o'er tropical scenes,
   I really had nae time tae spare,
But, noo, when I think o' ma kind-herted freens,
   I'm weel pleased wi wha I met there.

There I met wi George Spence, a miner o' sense,
    Wha wis manager aince at Newmains,
His guid wife and he made ma e'en kind o' dim;
    When they crack't o' lang syne and byganes.
They wur herty and hale, o' guid comp'ny the
        wale,
    And I enjoyed a treat that wis rare,
As we spak' o' Coltness, I am free tae confess
    I wished that I wis bodily thair.

Whin I wis a laddie I ne'er tried tae shine,
    If invited tae pairty, or ba'—
The lassies—a' times an attraction o' mine,
    And whiles ane mair sae than them a';
A rose-tinted cheek, a lauchin' blue e'e,
    Or a ringlet o' bricht gowden hair,
Wid haunt me fur days, pit ma mind in a haze,
    Wi wonderin' wha I'd meet thair.

When balmy spring melted the cauld winter
        snaws,
    And the hedges wur buddin' and green;
And the dark, swayin' pines wur the roosts o'
        the craws,
    When thae flew frae the ploughed fields at
        e'en;

In a lanesome bit walk doon by the burn side,
  Or a stroll through the streets wi thair glare,
Wi pretended surprise my joy whiles I hide
  When I meet some kent folks thair.

When death, that grim king, wha shall ca' fur me
    sune,
  And gie me short time tae prepare,
Grant, Lord that I may gang tae the mansions
    abune,
  I winder wha I'll meet up thair?
Fur ae thing I ken if I trust in the bluid
  And leeve my life here on the square,
Trying each day tae dae somebody guid,
  I'll meet my dear Saviour up thair.

The Shotts

A.D. 1802-1902.
Suggested by reading in the Hamilton Advertiser of the centenary of the Shotts Iron Works, and to J. W. Ormiston, Esq., for many years the general manager there, the following lines are most respectfully dedicated by the author.

It's a wild hilly countrie, sae bleak and sae bare,
Except fur th' heather that grows everywhere,
And a few bonnie wild flooers baith hardy and
     rare,
    That bloom in the lown boildy spots;
And yet it is richer than mair favor'd climes,
Wi its tales o' romance, and its auld warld
     rhymes,
And wha is't that hisna in modern times
    Heard tell o' the place ca'd the Shotts?

In the year ninety-ane, whin on a trip hame
Among ma dear freens and auld places again,
At Goodockhill ferm, my freen Mistress Gra-
     hame,
    Gied me a book o' Historic Notes"

By ane Doctor Grossart, 'tis written fu well,
And happy I'd been tae meet wi the chiel,
But I learned he had passed tae the land o' the
    leal,
   Ere I read his book on the Shotts.

Here in primitive times, I hae heard it declared,
Whin oor ancient forefaithers each had a yaird,
And muckle hard labour upon it thae waird,
   Tae cultivate baarly and oats;
But whin at Yuletide it wis still "green as a leek,"
(Tho' then Guid be thankit no polluted wi
    reek),
Thae thocht it high time somewhaur else thae
    should seek,
   For a fortune in ferms, than the Shotts.

But if tae the surface dame nature's unkind,
'Twas shin found that 'neath it wis rich treasure-
    lined,
And sae like douce men thae turned in and mined
   For the wealth in her deep-hidden grotts;
The staple industry at length it became,
And tho' it wis Omoa, saw the first furnace
    flame,
'Twas ne'er quite successful—perhaps 'twas the
    name—
   For ye ken that is foreign tae Shotts

Near the source o' the Calder ae fine efturnune,
Some geologist bodies (David Mosket was ane)
Wur takin' a walk whin he linger 't akin,
    Tae luk 'roond aboot him and slyly "tak'
        notes,"
And the longer he lukit on't, he like't it the mair,
For he saw baith coal and airnstane wur there,
"Sic a place fur an airnwark," quoth he, "I de-
        clare,
    I hae ne'er seen the like o' the Shotts."

It wis here that the airnwarks in eichteen and
        twa
First reflected thair glare in the sky's azure blue,
Aften since tae be cheenged tae a dark, murky
        hue,
    That the poets and penters ca' blots.
The skilled fellow-craftsmen assembled fu soon
And there by the calder sprang up the bit toon,
And noo tho' a hale hunder years hae past 'roon,
    It's a flourishin' place yet, the Shotts.

When I wis a bairnie in Bonkle I leeved,
And there my first lessons o' life I received,
And tho' ye may doot it, I've always believed
    In the story 'bout that wife o' Lots's;

For the hame she wis leavin', it seems she did
  yearn,
Day and nicht she did naethin' but yamer and
  girn,
Lukin' back she wis turned intae saut—'twad
  bin airn
 Had she happened tae leeve in the Shotts.

I hae leeved in this wurl' fur full fifty year,
'Midst its joys, its sorrows, its smiles and its
  tears,
And the ae magic word, ever sweet tae ma ears
 Is hame, wi its mem'ries and thochts;
It tiches ma hert like some "saft melodie"
That I've heard lang syne by a fond mother's
  knee,
And again I'm a bairn 'neath that humble rif-tree
 By the roadside no faur frae the Shotts.

To My Dog

"The More I See of Men the Better I Love Dogs."
—*Madame DeStael.*

He may have come of a mongrel breed,
    I know not his pedigree,
But that is a matter unworthy of heed,
    He is all that a dog should be;
On his faithfulness I can always depend,
    I have tried him and found him true,
And that much cannot be said of my friend,
    I doubt, about me and you.

He welcomes me home when I come from my
        work
    With the most exuberant joy,
And if his speech was as plain as his bark,
    I know he would say, "Old Boy,
I'm delighted to see, you're hungry and tired,
    But we'll have supper ready soon;
I'm at your service, and cannot be tired,
    Not even to 'bay at the moon.' "

He sits on the stair with a pensive air,
    And looks on the world around,
And growls a challenge to any who dare
    Disturb his studies profound;
With a faraway look in his honest brown eyes,
    That you never will see in a rogue,
On frail human nature, I whiles moralize,
    Then the better I love my dog.

When the evening is fine, I saunter abroad,
    He soberly walks by my side,
And he never betrays by a look or a nod,
    Any secrets in him I confide;
"My views" he will patiently hear to the end,
    And with them entirely agree,
Such courtesy cannot be said, my friend,
    I doubt about you or me.

His coat is curly and glossy and black,
    He knows every word that I say,
Ev'n if he could speak, he would never talk back
    I'm sure, in a short, saucy way;
He is quite content to stay with me
    And live on the humblest fare,
But the way he fawns, you can plainly see
    That he thinks I'm a millionaire.

His name is Rudolf—it sounds rather Dutch—
    But it's little he cares for that,
I am told by those who know "about such"
    That it's very aris-to-crat;
But bless his soul—I believe he has one—
    And a very big one, too,
And that after all is said and done,
    Makes him equal to me and you.

To the Tower o' Hall-Bar

This interesting old tower belongs to the Lockharts
of Lee, and is located near the village of Braidwood
in the parish of Carluke, Lanarkshire, Scotland. See
Murray's History of the Upper Ward of Lanarkshire.

'Tis an auld world relic so grim and so gray
    Half-hid 'mangst the foliage of fruit-laden
        trees,
And it tells us a tale of a bygone day,
    When the din of the battle swelled loud on the
        breeze;
Like a sentinel it stands o'er the fair pleasant
    lands,
    It seems to keep guard, looking out from afar,
As if ready to challenge all hostile
    That dare to approach the auld Tower o' Hall-
        Bar.

Oft times have I gazed on its time-worn walls
    And musingly thought of the men who lived
        there,
'Till fancy re-peopled those long silent halls
    With brave belted knights and bright ladies
        fair;
Did the troubadour sing to his lady-love
    'Neath the lattice, and touch the light guitar?
Or the crusader wear on his helmet a glove
    When he rode away from the Tower o' Hall-
        Bar?

Perchance from yon turret, with tear bedimmed
    eye,
    She watched her brave lover recede from her
        view,
Away to the south where the bold mountains
    rise,
    He halted to wave her a long, sad adieu;
Ah, the long years of waiting, so sadly and
    wearily,
    How often the landscape she scanned from
        afar,
If haply she might see the knight she loved
    dearly
    Returning to her and the Tower o' Hall-Bar.

Close by the glen where the brackens grow
    green,
  And the wee burnie sings on its way to the
    Clyde,
Full oft in the moonlight, 'tis said may be seen
  The ghosts of a lady and knight side by side.
And this is the legend the villagers tell——.
  That the brave cavalier ne'er returned from
    the war,
But nightly his spirit keeps tryst in the dell
  With his dear lady-love of the Tower o' Hall-
    Bar.

Mary's Sunday Gown

It is not made of costly silk,
  Nor ivory satin rare;
It is not trimmed with old point lace
  That ladies like to wear.
I'm sure that you would call it plain,
  And yet no belle in town
Looks half so sweet as Mary,
  When she wears her Sunday gown.

Perhaps you've met with Mary,
  She works upon the farm,
A winsome little fairy
  Of artless grace and charm.
Her little hands with toil are hard,
  Her cheeks are ruddy brown,
But, she's "princess of the boulevard"
  Dressed in her Sunday gown.

'Tis sometimes scant in longitude,
    And thus her ankles neat
Attract the eyes of "mashers" rude
    Who throng the city street;   1
But like some sweet wild violet,
    Demurely looking down,
She's peerless in her toilet
    When she wears her Sunday gown.

She goes to church, the little elf,
    A worshipper sincere,
She does not go to show herself,
    Nor mark what others wear;
But Tommy Green, he calls her "Queen,"
    (She calls him "lout" and "clown")
Because there is "too much a screen"
    'Bout Mary's Sunday gown.

Amongst the list of "fashion's set"
    Her name you will not find;
In what is known as "etiquette"
    She is perhaps behind.
She's just a simple country lass,
    Unversed in ways "high-flown,"
But the flowers look up to see her pass
    Dressed in her Sunday gown.

When Pa Brought Home His Check

My pa was idle most a year,
  He could find naught to do,
And with us kids and mammy dear,
  I tell you things looked blue.
But now he's got a trammer's job,
  'Tis steady I expeck—
My! we were proud (tho' Ma did sob)
  When pa brought home his check.

I tell you it was pretty tough,
  We scarce had 'nough to eat,
The weather, too, was could and rough,
  The shoes worn off our feet;
We rustled coal and kindling wood,
  There'd been a railroad wreck,
But now we've lots of all things good,
  Since pa brought home his check.

Then every night, soon after dark,
  Ma sent us off to bed,
And little Tom and Rob and Mark,
  They used to cry for bread.
Then ma, she used to tell us how
  The Lord would not negleck
To feed His flock—less danger now,
  Since pa brought home his check.

When little sister Lizzie died,
  The youngest and the pet,
We buried her in Sunnyside,
  And had to go in debt;
We couldn't 'ford to buy a wreath
  Her little grave to deck,
But it won't be forgotten now
  Since pa brought home his check.

I'm growing bigger every day,
  I'll soon be leavin' school,
And when I start to work for pay,
  You bet I'll be no fool;
Then ma will laugh and cry for joy,
  And hug me 'round the neck,
And call me her own darling boy,
  When I bring home my check.

The Land of the West

After the style of emigration touters.

Now rouse ye, my brothers across the sea,
  And leave the old land behind,
Dear tho' its memories be to thee,
  And by many fond ties entwined;
Ah, the tear-drops fall as I think of you all
  With hunger and want opprest,
Whilst there's plenty here, of the best of cheer,
  In this beautiful land of the west.

Oh, come find a home where the buffaloes roam,
  The deer and the antelope,
And the sun shines bright from morning till night,
  On the rocky mountain's slope.
Oh, how grandly they rise—you'd look with
    surprise
  On Pike's Peak with its snow-laden crest;
Oh, we've all kinds of weather all blended to-
    gether
  In this picturesque land of the west.

115

If your tastes are for farming, what life is more
      charming
    Than to live by tilling the soil?
The prairie is wide on every side,
    It stretches for many a mile.
Just get some barbed wire, that is all you require,
    And fence in what e'er you think best;
Whatever you sow, it is sure to grow
    In the fertile land of the west.

The cactus, the soapwood and sageweed grow,
    The cedar and mountain pine,
And flowers whose names I really don't know.
    Clear above the timber line;
The grass—well, it's short, and yet I do think
    It is surely not hard to digest,
For the cattle are meek, contented and sleek,
    In this beautiful land of the west.

Should you court the shy dame—the prospect-
      ing game,
    You may strike it rich any day;
If silver and gold you don't find in your "claim"
    You are certain of gravel and clay;
It is hard to advise, no matter how wise,
    As to where, when, or how to invest,
With all honour due, this is nowhere more true
    Than in this lovely land of the west.

We have churches galore, and excellent schools,
    And amusements of every kind;
We have all kinds of men—sages and fools,
    Where can you a better place find?
With our mixed population, a unique combina-
        tion,
    We're happy, it must be confest,
For life is so cheery, no one could feel dreary,
    In this wonderful land of the west.

Then why longer toil, like African slaves,
    In the workshop, the mill and the mine,
And perchance in the end to fill pauper's graves,
    Leaving your loved ones in poverty to pine.
Ah, the tear-drops fall when I think of you all,
    With tyrannical masters opprest,
Whilst there's plenty of everything good out
        here,
    In this glorious land of the west.

Here's to You, Jim

Here's to you, Jim, you've proved a
  friend,
  Our grateful thanks we owe you,
We're pleased to see this trouble end,
  And better now we know you.
A gentleman—you've met us fair,
  In friendly consultation,
You merit and receive your share
  Of warmest approbation.

Here's to you, Jim, if in the past
  There's been misunderstanding,
The stormiest voyage ends at last,
  With greater joyous landing;
When murky clouds obscure the sky
  The lightning flash can clear it,
When to the rocks some ship is nigh,
  Some skillful hand must steer it.

Here's to you, Jim, you did not need
    The aid of thugs with rifles,
Tho' well you knew we never heed
    Such unimportant trifles.
But you're the "hero of the hour"
    (I read that in the papers),
Oh, if you had the Gov'nor's power,
    You'd soon stop all these capers.

Here's to you, Jim, in sparkling wine,
    Or if you wish it—water,
A humble, homely muse is mine
    That never aims to flatter;
But still we wish some we could name
    From you would take a lesson,
The "Overall Brigade" looks tame,
    With aye a Sunday dress on.

Here's to you, Jim, the best of luck,
    We hope will still attend you,
Be sure we will not see you stuck
    For aught we can befriend you.
You've stood by us, we'll stand by you,
    No more a fence divides us,
So here's to Burns, mine, mill and crew
    Until the green sod hides us.

Jimmie Shut Her Down

James Burns, president and general manager of the Portland Gold Mining Company, at Victor, Col., in 1901, had a misunderstanding with the miners' union, and to show his authority shut down the mine for two weeks. By his subsequent conduct Mr. Burns regained the respect of the miners.

Oh, what a dire calamity,
    Has fallen on us now,
The Portland mine it has shut down,
    I can't tell why or how.
There is silence on the mountain,
    And there's sorrow in the town,
And gold is scarce in Europe
    Since Jimmie shut her down.

The tangled Chinese question
    Of late has caused a din,
The basis that it rests on
    Is displeasing to Ah Sin;
The Russian bear is growling,
    And der Kaiser wears a frown,
And Johnny Bull is growling
    Since Jimmie shut her down.

The international yacht race
　　They say has been postponed,
And Morgan' to the British has
　·　Three hundred millions loaned;
His royal majesty, Eddie,
　　They say has pawned his crown,
And wants to swap with Teddy,
　　Since Jimmy shut her down.

There's a flurry in the market,
　　And stocks are selling low,
The future it looks dark yet,
　　But 'twill not be always so;
For the dark cloud has a lining
　　(Tho' unfit for lady's gown,)
And the sun has kept on shining
　　Since Jimmy shut her down.

Farewell, My Mountain Home

Farewell to thee, my mountain home,
    Where twenty years of life I've spent;
Farewell, and may the time soon come
    When gentle peace and sweet content
Shall bless this pleasant land again,
    As it was blessed in happiest times,
'Ere blighted by a tyrant's reign,
    Curs'd with his cruelties and crimes.

Farewell to thee, my mountain home,
    Ye winds that sway the somber pines,
Scent-laden with the sweet arome
    Of guelder-rose and columbines.
Preserve the bloom on beauty's cheek,
    And cool the feverish brow of care;
Relieve the suffering and the weak,
    But poison every traitor there.

Farewell to thee, my mountain home,
　　In manhood's prime I came to thee;
By honest toil my bread I've won,
　　And bent to none a servile knee.
Always within my "cable tow"
　　By "compass points" I've tried to steer;
Too old to learn a new "chart" now,
　　When to the port I'm drawing near.

Farewell to thee, my mountain home,
　　Perhaps for years—perhaps for aye—
Farewell, my friends—I still have some,
　　I hope to meet again some day;
Elsewhere another home I'll seek
　　Where honest men may still be free,
Not cringing slaves, afraid to speak,
　　My mountain home, farewell to thee.

Mr. John McNeil, M. E.

To a Rhyming Brother, Mr. John McNeil, M. E.,
Inspector of Mines, Denver, Cal.

I sit doon tae write ye man, Johnnie McNeil,
And tae answer invite ye man, Johnnie McNeil,
Tho' humble my muse and but limpin' atweel,
She's aye cantie and croose man, Johnnie Mc-
    Neil.

There's a land over the sea man, Johnnie McNeil,
Whaur the brave and the free man, Johnnie
    McNeil,
Aft in war's crimson tide, have conquered and
    died,
But ne'er turned aside man, Johnnie McNeil.

'Tis the land o' sweet song man, Johnnie McNeil,
'Tis the land we proudly own man, Johnnie Mc-
    Neil,
Her grand lofty bens, and her deep bosky glens,
Ilka true Scotsman kens man, Johnnie McNeil.

Then here's tae auld Scotland, man, Johnnie
   McNeil,
And her heroes—a noble band—Johnnie Mc-
   Neil,
Whaur the dark heather waves o'er the martyrs'
   lone graves,
There's nae coowards or slaves, man, Johnnie
   McNeil.

CPSIA information can be obtained
at www.ICGtesting.com
Printed in the USA
BVHW071209201218
536078BV00015B/269/P